Maximising Individual Wealth

The Digital Age Handbook

William Houston

ADVFN BOOKS

Contents

Introduction   1
Chapter 1. Background to the New Employment Structures   7
Chapter 2. New Opportunities for Individual Employment
    and Investment   31
Chapter 3. Technology Investment Driving the Digital Age   45
Chapter 4. The New Corporation   51
Chapter 5. The Structures of the New Paradigm   59
Addendum   65
References   70
About the Author   72
Reviews of William Houston's Other Books   74

Introduction

The Digital Era will enter the world like a constructive dynamic wind lasting perhaps half a generation, taking much of the present increasingly redundant state superstructure with it.

Those who have read and understood this handbook will be able to make wise prior dispositions of their career and wealth. The others will be taken care of in a highly constructive programme designed to make each individual a respected member of society.

The wind is being driven by two powerful forces: debt and technology.

We can see the mountain that must be climbed by reviewing the amount of debt relative to America's total output by studying Diagram 1 which sets out this ratio from 1870 to the near present. It comes by courtesy of Hoisington Investment Management of Austin, Texas.

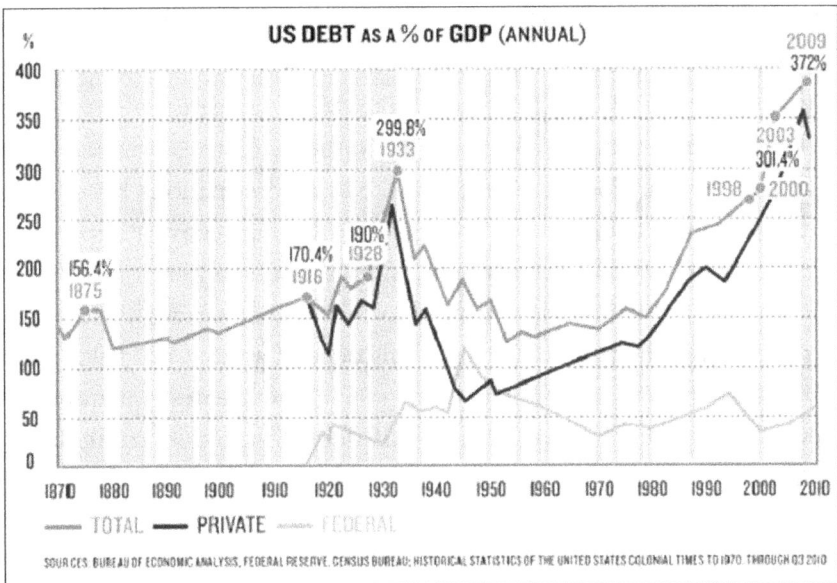

The reader will discern a pattern of around 50 to 70 years which goes back to around 1790, of which the latest two cycles, and the start of the present, are shown; the end of the second rhythm was in 1880, the third in 1950. We can learn something of what lies ahead by tracing the movement of the third cycle from its start in around 1890 then its rise to 1929 when the debt/GDP was around 200% and the unemployment figure was 4.2%.

But in 1929 things went horribly wrong. Through various gross policy errors and the large overhanging private debt shown in green, the economic output declined by 50% in the years to 1932 and unemployment rose to nearly 25%. From 1930 debt started to collapse, taking with it about half of the 22,000 banks and many other enterprises. Despite strenuous efforts to alleviate unemployed through the Roosevelt New Deal, those out of work stayed stubbornly above 17% throughout the 1930s while private debt collapsed. It was only during the magnificent war effort that unemployment fell to 1.2% in 1944.

The present economic cycle started in 1950 and the debt/GDP ratio stayed reasonably low until 1980 when a combination of a rise of public and private debt saw the ratio starting to rise rapidly and unemployment increased to around 7%. Over the next decades the ratio rose to 273% in 2009 and by 2016 it is nearer 400% – and unless drastic action is taken, it will continue to rise, bringing on a major recession. The US is not alone. Most other nations have ratios better or worse and history shows that no lasting recovery is possibly unless the debt/GDP ratio is reduced to 200% or lower.

We now have some background to the present which, if the future is to resemble the past, means that this debt of at least $20 trillion has to be lost in the US, for it is evident that the greatest quantity will never be repaid. The two methods of debt destruction are deflation and inflation. The Americans tried the first in the 1930s, the Germans suffered the second in the early 1920s; neither country is determined to repeat their history, which destroyed livelihoods and savings and in Germany saw the rise of Adolf Hitler!

Whatever method is tried, one may be sure that unemployment will rise dramatically and dealing with it is one of the prime objectives for this handbook; the other is to identify the investment opportunities in the new era of the Digital Age. For how the recovery is managed – see the **Global Recovery Manual***.

The Second Dynamic is Technology

A recent Oxford University study concluded that computerised technology would replace 47% of jobs in 400 occupations in the US within decades. This comes on the realisation that future employment patterns will, at best, need a large minority to become self-employed with some reduction of living standards, but their reward will be the control over their own destiny. At this point we can identify just a few of the areas where technology will replace people or allow them to be performed by non-professionals – see *The Future of the Professions****.

- Hospitals are now using robots to deliver medicines around to the wards with great precision. At the same time the need for highly qualified staff is being increasingly overtaken by para-professionals using sophisticated diagnostic equipment.

- Legal firms are breaking down more sophisticated tasks into modules that may be completed by para-professionals using a huge range of web-based services. Legal disputes are now being settled by computer based services that can very swiftly analyse the principles on which a dispute can be resolved.

- Technology allows many back-office services to be served remotely by specialist groups while at the same time keeping instant communication; this considerably reduces commuting transport and wear and tear on individuals. This technique is being used by consulting firms referring to specialist agencies rather than costly in-house libraries.

- In the US, sophisticated line tax services allow individuals to prepare their returns much more readily and cheaply than using an advisor. In accounting it has been the practice in an audit to sample data manually, now specialist programs have been written to pick out inconsistencies and errors in virtually all the accounting entries.

The combination of solving the debt crisis, described earlier, and the technological revolution will place tremendous pressures on those affected at all levels of society as they will be obliged to adjust very rapidly to a new equilibrium; it will also present problems to investors whose savings will need to be directed away from uncertain stock markets into sound and profitable venues. Unemployment will increasingly become a problem.

By the end of 2015 there were nearly 30 million unemployed in Europe which was over 10% of the workforce. Of these well over five million (some 22%) were under 25 – half of these in Greece, Spain and Italy. Although there are support programmes in all countries, this appalling state is already heralding extreme right-wing nationalistic movements in several countries, as they did in the 1930s. More will follow. Programmes, such as those suggested in this handbook, will be essential to avoid revolutions in several countries.

These concerns are addressed by this handbook which covers the transition from a condition where the state dominates many facets of life into an individual-led revolution by providing an essential linkage from the present to the future in five chapters:

- The new measures to correct this appalling unemployment situation are described in Chapter 1 under the heading of the Conservation and Security Agency (CSA), modelled on

Roosevelt's Civilian Conservation Corps (CCC). This was a programme set up in March 1933 to employ young men in environmental work in camps around the USA. The CSA mobilises all those on state support into a constructive work and training plan designed to bring many of those without work into self-employment.

- New opportunities for the self-employed with their associated investment opportunities are suggested in Chapter 2, for there will be many openings for new enterprises, particularly in the newly privatised public services, as governments are obliged to reduce costs as described in the *Global Recovery Manual**. As different layers of support are provided, these are likely to be funded by different forms of venture capital, often through linkages with other nations.

- Some of the new technologies are described in Chapter 3, for difficult times not only accelerate the demand for existing technologies but are the driving force for new ones because of the need to create new products to attract buyers – who can delay to buy the same item more cheaply later. After the destruction of many financial organisations in the conditions described earlier, new venture capital vehicles will arise to fund the new industries to develop the new ideas.

- Chapter 4 describes some of the new corporate structures, for although there will still be large process-style companies, there will be a much greater number of small specialised firms either acting as sub-contractors such as the German *Mittelstand* or satisfying a rising demand for specific products. These will range from the ability to produce such items as bespoke apparel, furniture, bicycles – or even cars. The new structures will be controlled by more owner/managers than before and be located in regions which offer the greatest business, education, social, financial and cultural support.

Not only will businesses need changing their formats but the need for governments to reduce their costs to around 30% of GDP will demand a much more devolved style of administration as found in Switzerland. Chapter 5 and the associated Addendum will emphasise the importance of regions or states as they configure themselves to attract new business in a similar manner to Swiss cantons. As was evident in previous hard times, individuals, either singly or in groups, will provide the driving force and innovation in the new Digital Age so ably described in *The Sovereign Individual*****.

A Reflection on Our Approach to the Digital Age

The aim of this handbook is to help us navigate our way through a major discontinuity before arriving at a more peaceful destination. Historians will judge whether we made wise dispositions and helped others not so gifted as ourselves.

Chapter 1.
Background to the New Employment Structures

Summary

This chapter aims to show how many individuals, from varied backgrounds and displaced either by technology or economic distress, can regain their feet and create a new life. It explores many past initiatives and how the best of these may be adapted to the future that will lead to investment opportunities.

Introduction

By mid-2016 it is evident that few politicians have a true understanding of the economic and climatic perils facing their nation. Neither do they seem to grasp the policies associated with deflation except in general terms. This is a tragedy because the rapid advent of the Digital Age (DA) will present them with the prospect of rising unemployment that could extend to over 45% in the transition; something that would lead, unless foreseen and anticipated, to civil unrest – even revolution.

At the same time the ability of the state to underwrite idleness is rapidly diminishing during a recession so alternatives must be found – almost certainly, for many, in self-employment. This is along the lines of the futurist Alvin Toffler who foresaw, in his book *The Third Wave*, a sort of high-tech dispersal of talent present in the Guilds of the 17th century before the concentration of the Industrial Age.

Furthermore, there will be many who would normally have thought of retirement but whose income will have been depleted by political action to devalue the currency in the hope of staving off deflation. Altogether any programme will probably need to incorporate more than one third of the population until a new equilibrium can be found.

This chapter sets out the background to any support programme and suggests how this may be implemented at minimum cost, but first it is important to evaluate the likely employment patterns of the Digital Era which could be set out under five headings:

- Manufacturing 10%
- Supporting services 40%
- Government 2%
- Agriculture 2%
- Self-employment 46%

The high proportion of self-employment arises from the twin forces described in the Introduction of debt deflation and technology that will lead to a rapid shake-out of traditional employment patterns over the relatively short time-scale of a generation or less. This will ensure a very rapid reduction of taxed income that will oblige governments to reduce costs along the lines set out in the *Global Recovery Manual** and, unless the measures described in this chapter are implemented, this will cause the major social problems suggested earlier. But before these can be implemented we first need to understand the legacy of the welfare state.

The Human Cost of the Welfare State

A study in April 2007 by The London School of Economics showed there were 1.2 million people in Britain who are what they called NEETs (not in education, employment or training) – twice that of

Germany and France; to this end deflation has probably added another million unfortunates. The report estimated that this cost the taxpayer £3.65 billion a year to which a statement from the Royal Bank of Scotland added £1 billion for the cost of crime and £18 billion for a lifetime of lost earnings. In all, the lack of political initiative cost the taxpayer $20 billion in 2007 which would be well over £40 billion by 2016.

Some of those classed as NEETs would include between two and three million children (between 10 and 15% of homes) living in houses without anyone being in work – something that could only increase as the recession described in the Introduction takes hold. There are also around over three million claiming disability allowances.

Quite apart from the welfare state being progressively unable to support them as government revenues decline, there is the human cost to the nation of up to 10% of the unemployed being debarred from making any contribution to the social or economic life of the country.

These people whom politicians have 'swept under the table' as being too difficult to deal with can be just accommodated in economical good times through transfer payments and policing. But with a major downturn, these unfortunates could be left to their own devices leading to an unacceptable increase of crime such as gang-wars in America, stabbings in Britain and riots in France. Without a sense of guidance some of the least advantaged could become radicalised to make terrorist attacks on a society that has chosen not to listen – this is quite apart from so-called 'martyrs' whom some cleric has encouraged to believe that paradise awaits those who kill innocent infidels.

This potential employment time-bomb is not singular to Britain, it is bound to hit all westernised countries where a radical decline in the prospect of producing such commoditised products as cars, computers and other manufactured goods will generate levels of unemployment not seen for 80 or so years.

How to navigate a large minority of the population through an extremely difficult period which will see differentials of income widen dramatically is today's problem – and a new opportunity to provide the means to value the individual.

Employing those out of work stems back at least to Ancient Egypt when farmers, unable to till their land while the Nile flooded, were put to work building pyramids and temples. While the skilled building and fashioning work was done by masons, engravers, plasterers and painters, the humping was an unskilled task relegated to the farmers. The manhandling work on the tombs and monuments stopped when the river subsided and it was time to plant seed once again.

In biblical times Jesus showed how individuals could be responsible to two masters. When asked whether it was lawful to pay taxes to the Romans he asked his interviewer to produce a denarius which had the face of Caesar on one side. Jesus replied, give unto Caesar what is his due and God what is His.

A similar duality which did not involve loyalties was adopted early in the 13th century when the great cathedrals were built in France, England and Italy during what is known as the Medieval Warming. There was then adequate rainfall, the crops yielded a good harvest, and the farmers were recruited to handle the heavy work. Remarkably for the period, Salisbury Cathedral was built over some 35 years in a period of good growing weather. Building slowed in the early decades of the next century when poor weather required the farmers to till even the poorer land. It virtually stopped during the black death 20 years later to be revived later with the much plainer Perpendicular Gothic.

200 years on, the first Poor Laws were passed in England in 1597/8 and 1601 to help those made destitute by the appalling weather when the population had just recovered to the same level as before the *great dying* – as the Black Death was known. The responsibility to organise help was delegated to the church wardens

who were required to house and put the destitute to work in the fields while apprenticeships were found for the children.

So successful was this programme that it was copied in many other countries. It continued to be a charitable issue in England until 1834 when the cost of support was so great that stringent admission requirements were introduced to admit only the demonstrably needy to the workhouses.

Although the Industrial Revolution created many jobs there was a major work hiatus in Germany late in the 19th century when industrialisation took place over a generation – compared to four generations in Britain. Fearing civil unrest Otto von Bismarck, the German Chancellor in the latter part of the 19th century, introduced a mild form of the welfare state to provide help for those who suffered the most. His ideas were taken up and expanded by Lloyd George of the Liberal government in Britain in the early 20th century; a process that curtailed many charitable organisations.

The next serious attempts to alleviate unemployment were made during the 1930s in Germany and America for very different reasons: in the former, as a prelude to re-armament, in the latter as a make-work programme to deal with jobless figures of 25%. It is worth examining these to help formulate future plans.

Italy and Germany

When Mussolini became the Italian dictator in 1922 he seemed initially quite tolerant of industrialists – while they still paid their taxes – and spent money on the infrastructure such as roads and building sport stadiums; these were good times of full employment. All this changed in the early 1930s when, in an effort to reduce people being laid off, he organised a state holding company that bought into failing companies. His task was helped by re-armament for his adventures in Abyssinia, Libya and the Balkans.

By contrast, when Adolf Hitler became Chancellor on 30 January 1933, the country's unemployment was six million, the economy was stagnant, banks had failed and many feared a communist revolution. Some two years later, the jobless total was around 600.000, economic output was at pre-slump figures and inflation had been contained.

This remarkable performance, which surpassed anything achieved in a democracy (and which would never have been acceptable in one) was due to several basic principles. Among them were the Nazi election pledges to build a road infrastructure, to make Germany as self-sufficient as possible in food and a requirement to make people physically fit after a period of inaction.

All this was made possible by ruthlessly eliminating trade unions and political opposition, introducing financial controls that funded work programmes without inflation and a rigid fascist control of every element of society. There was, of course, a downside. Prices and wages were rigidly controlled, individuals were not allowed to leave the land for better pay elsewhere and enterprise was severely directed towards state objectives.

While this was going on the mark was kept steady by strictly controlling foreign exchange for essential raw materials; this was helped by negotiating bi-lateral deals with countries like Romania exchanging oil for manufactured items. To help Germany to be self-sufficient in oil, research was initiated to produce synthetic oil using the Fischer Tropsch Process and to obtain rubber from coal. Later, when Roosevelt criticised Hitler for re-armament, the Fuhrer retorted reasonably that his remedial programme had been infinitely more successful than that of America's in creating work.

The United States

In March 1933 the new president Franklin D Roosevelt's first task was to halt bank failures by calling a 'holiday'; his next act would prove to be inspired. On 21 March 1933 he sent to Congress the following proposal:

'A Civilian Conservation Corps (CCC) that would be used in simple work, not interfering with normal employment, and confining itself to forestry, the prevention of soil erosion, flood control and similar projects. More important however than the material gains will be the moral and spiritual value of such work. The Americans who are now walking the streets and receiving private and public relief would infinitely prefer to work. We can take a vast army of unemployed out in to healthy surroundings. We eliminate, to some extent, the threat that enforced idleness brings to spiritual and moral stability. It is not a panacea but I estimate that 250,000 men can be given temporary employment by the early summer if you will give me the authority to proceed within the next two weeks.'

He got it by 31 March.

The countryman in Roosevelt told him there was clearly useful work to be done by some of the five million unemployed young men in the millions of farmland acres being eroded. In addition huge areas were threatened by fire, and regions like the Shenandoah Mountains were being made barren by indiscriminate logging for fuel. Instead of creating a new ministry, he set up an advisory council directed by Robert Fechner, a labour leader from Boston, that included representatives from the departments of Defense, Agriculture and the Interior. The idea was to open camps to be run by the armed services and the work to be supervised and training given by 'local experienced men' (LEMs).

The initial call was for 240,000 unmarried young men between the ages of 18 and 25, who had completed eight years of schooling and were from families on relief. The first call was not well supported but, after clearing away bureaucratic hurdles, 275,000 young men and First World War veterans had been recruited. Individuals were to be paid $30 a month of which $22 was to be sent home and there were bonus payments of up to $5 for undertaking special duties such as leading gangs, working in the cook-house and so on. The first task was to send the volunteers to special camps where they underwent two or three weeks of nutritional and physical conditioning before they were fit enough to work.

By September 1935, enrolment had peaked at over 500,000, the recruits serving in over 2,500 camps and by 1938 over two million men had served. Once the pattern had been set, Fechner introduced education and training into the curriculum and reduced the lower age limit to 17.

The results were impressive. Nearly 90,000 miles of telephone lines had been rigged, almost 3,500 fire towers built, more than six million days were spent fighting fires, and nearly 70,000 miles of fire-breaks dug. Other work included planting more than two billion trees, building flood protection, making footpaths, restoring woodland and forests, aiding soil conservation, working in disaster relief and restoring historic areas such as battlefields. This work was not without danger; although sound training was given, 29 men died fighting fires, ten of them in the Shoshone National forest in Wyoming.

The CCC did not just help young men do worthwhile work, it also gradually increased the educational content as many men had dropped out of school. From 1934, an education advisor was authorised for each camp and local teachers were enlisted as volunteers to help 40,000 who could not read or write. Much of the training was vocational, such as car and truck maintenance, forestry, the handling of heavy equipment, carpentry, welding, the use of radios and so on. In addition people could study subjects such as journalism, surveying, photography and psychology, backed up by correspondence courses. When war was declared, the CCC turned over most of its camps to the army and the programme was disbanded in mid-1942 – after providing some nine years of valuable service. The CCC also helped to reduce crime; a Chicago judge commented that the program was largely responsible for a 55% reduction of crime by young men.

The CCC was the most successful programme of the New Deal but there were others such as the Work Program Administration (WPA) as a means of creating work for men who would otherwise be on the dole. Like the CCC, the work should not conflict with commercial operations and only one member of a family was allowed to take part. Although the WPA got a name for digging holes in the ground then filling them up again it did succeed in building, renovating, tidying-up or repairing 20,000 public areas such as playgrounds, hospitals, schools and airfields. In doing this it achieved Roosevelt's aim of providing people with much greater satisfaction than being idle, but the programme was not continuous and, unlike the CCC, it lacked incentives for taking more responsibility or learning additional skills.

Britain

The 1931 coalition government generated a business friendly environment that created boom conditions in the Midlands and south-east but no job creation programmes to help the deprived areas. There was major hardship among the staple industries of coal, iron, shipbuilding and textiles in Wales, North England and Scotland that generated its own unhappy legacy.

During The Second World War Britain introduced several potent quasi-voluntary organisations that could be useful guides to the present. The first was the Royal Observer Corps who manned visual aircraft spotting observation points around the coast and inland as a back-up to the Chain Home radar stations in case these were bombed or jammed. Next there were the Air Raid Wardens who were trained to guard public buildings such as St Paul's against incendiary bombs, to spot breaches in the black-out, to put out fires and to help bring people to safety.

Probably the most interesting was the Home Guard set up by Winston Churchill after the evacuation from Dunkirk in 1940. Originally armed with nothing more than pitchforks and shotguns, this gradually became a properly armed and trained force acting as a back-up to the army in case of invasion. They knew their locality, guarded essential buildings, bridges, power stations and so on. Some were trained as a fifth column in case of enemy occupation.

Ingredients for a Latter-day Employment and Welfare Programme

We can now identify the programmes that meet the needs set out earlier and policies that work and those that do not. History brought up to date shows us what should be done:

- Individuals working either singly or in groups bring a democratic economy out of recession, not the state; the best politicians can do it to create a stable currency, cut any restrictions to enterprise, encourage entrepreneurs with ideas for new activities and provide protection, where necessary, from imports dumped from abroad.

- Any recovery should include a spiritual element confirming the belief that individuals would be much better working constructively than being idle. In the early decades of the 21st century any programme must include defence against religious terrorism.

- The concept of the CCC should be a model for any new make-work plan. At its lowest level it should provide useful work for relatively simple but necessary local tasks, reward for responsibility and skills, remedial education and a counselling service. Experience shows it would help to reduce violence, truancy, and act as a back-up for dysfunctional families.

- Part of the programme should help to bring 'status zero' people and children back into the mainstream – their existence is an indictment on the state, the churches and society.

- A modern CCC could use an organisation such as the Guardian Angels – described later – to help the police and security services to guard against terrorist attacks, patrolling school grounds against marauders and drug dealers, helping to reduce violence on the streets and transport, and acting as vigilantes as a support for law enforcement.

- The educational element is important for much of employment creation will be for self-employment.

- At the national and international level there will be an increasing need for individuals to be trained in disaster relief from incidents such as earthquakes, flooding, tsunamis, refugees and so on. This might be a semi-military force, along the lines of the Swiss citizens army described later. Many of these individuals could later join the armed forces as the need for military support increases.

- The local programmes should be managed by voluntary organisations and paid with funds normally set aside as unemployment or incapacity benefit. In addition there would be revenue from work done by individuals and groups contracting these services – see TCV below.

- National programmes should be managed by the military.

- The German experience taught the importance of individual health and fitness.

- Welfare help for those not immediately absorbed by work-creation programmes should be decentralised and administered locally just as the first Poor Laws were administered in the Late Elizabethan period and the Wisconsin's W2 described in the *Global Recovery Manual**.

- Any programmes should have the effect of reducing crime as was the experience of the CCC.

- Anyone can leave the programme for gainful work.

The policies that do not work:

- Paying for people to do nothing. This includes those suffering from a range of disabilities, single parents and those apparently looking for work, see the W-2 initiative.

- One-off work generating plans do not fulfil the need.

- The New Deal's Public Works Administration (PWA) was excellent for achieving big project benefits to the infrastructure but employed relatively few people. Japan emulated Roosevelt's New Deal in the 1990s and succeeding in building roads and railways that led nowhere which generated a large budget deficit, big borrowings but were no cure for unemployment.

The next sections suggest how a *Latter-Day CCC* could probably be grafted on to existing voluntary organisations at local and national level in the UK – other nations may have some of their own initiatives. Among these examples are the National Trust, the Trust for Conservation Volunteers, the Guardian Angels, the Defense 2eme Chance in France and the Swiss Army. At some level it would be sensible for national programmes to be managed by the armed forces who, by their nature, are skilled at training and organising large numbers of people. All these, in their own ways, could help to meet the objectives set out earlier.

The National Trust

The NT in Britain was founded in 1895 to 'preserve places of historic interest or natural beauty permanently for the nation to enjoy'. Being independent of the government it relies on the generosity of its supporters through membership subscriptions, gifts, legacies, the contribution of over 35,000 volunteers; it charges for admission. It owns around 612,000 acres of the most beautiful countryside and almost 600 miles of coastline. It has in its care over 200 historic houses and gardens and nearly 50 industrial monuments and mills.

While all the managing staff are salaried, there are a large number of opportunities for volunteers. For example, in the Thames and Solent region there are clerical openings in the departments of fund-raising, marketing, education, exhibitions, historic building guides and box-office staff that can absorb talents of all ages and abilities and disabilities.

Before joining, volunteers receive an induction programme which includes such matters as the role of the NT, health, safety, and first aid. The remainder of the training is working alongside professional staff before becoming fully-fledged. There are, however, openings for long-term volunteers who contract to give 21 hours a week for at least three months. These may be undergraduates wishing to complement their own specialisations with practical and supervised work.

The Trust for Conservation Volunteers

TCV was set-up in the 1950s as a British Conservation Corps that was expanded in the 1960s to include education and training. The idea was developed in the 1970s by opening offices around mainland Britain and Northern Ireland and it became TCV with a head office in Doncaster.

Unlike the NT, TCV is obliged to charge for its services and its clients are widespread; among them are farmers, councils, local or national park supervisors, schools, the Ministry of Defence and commercial organisations. A project is initiated when a potential client calls upon someone in a local office (150 in nine regions). It is then assessed whether it is suitable for volunteers and if so, the job is costed. If the proposal is accepted it will be scheduled either locally or nationally depending upon the size and scope. Some work may require heavy equipment in which case the volunteers work alongside the contractors. Great care is taken not to engage in work that might otherwise be undertaken commercially.

Like the CCC, TCV has a spiritual element of inspiring people to enjoy transforming places that might otherwise go untended and improving the lives of those living in devastated areas of inner cities. It also aims to enrich the lives of over a million people by providing voluntary opportunities that will improve their health and education.

Most of the projects are countryside and environmentally-based, such as planting trees, clearing overgrown woodland, maintaining national parks and nature reserves. Among urban projects was one in Lambeth in London where volunteers worked to clear a distressed site, levelled it, planted trees and constructed gardens and playgrounds; the maintenance has now been taken over by the residents. Other city work includes working within communities to help relationships, reducing drug-taking and violence, cleaning up the streets and improving citizenship. Up to 40% of the urban projects are engaged in clearing waste land and canals, planting trees, repairing buildings and so on.

More recently, TCV has established overseas links with similar organisations. For example, in the year ending 31 March 2005 they organised 70 holidays in 23 countries including Kenya and Gambia; in the former volunteers supported the Colobus Trust helping to conserve endangered primates. This activity is growing and there are plans for further linkages.

The Guardian Angels

This group was set up by Curtis Silwa in New York City during 1979. Silwa was the manager of the East Fordham Road McDonald's frequented by many Puerto Rican youths. He originally set out to clean up garbage in the street then later to combat the widespread violence and crime in the city's subways. Its members, dressed in T-shirts, red jackets and berets, were trained to make citizen's arrests – an action that attracted public praise and official criticism, who accused them of being naive vigilantes causing more trouble than good.

The Angels' action precipitated a deep social and political debate about the role of government and the citizen in society and in due course led to moves by the authorities to involve people more closely in their communities. This led to the Angels improving their training with an emphasis on safety that led to better relations with the police and by the mid-1990s Mayor Rudolph Guiliani had become their most loyal supporter.

By the new century the Angels were running Safety Patrols, walking the streets or riding on public transport and, by encouraging people to become more involved, to help to make streets safer. Although they can make citizens arrests, their main focus is to deter crime and drug-dealing and their work has led them to schools where they help teachers deal with unruly behaviour, patrol playgrounds, deter bullies and keep watch over entrances. In addition the CyberAngels have been initiated to track down paedophiles, educate children and parents and set out safety rules for the vulnerable of the 205 million Americans who regularly use the internet.

The organisation is now run by Mary Silwa, an executive with a proven managerial record, who is concentrating on increasing professionalism, fund-raising, training and integrating the group both into society, and with the authorities. The Angels recruit from a wide range of age, ethnic and social backgrounds and there is a screening process that excludes previous trouble-makers. Apart from the USA, it now has 'chapters' in Japan, the United Kingdom, South Africa, Canada and has groups in some of the toughest cities in the world.

Defense 2eme Chance

This is an imaginative initiative launched by the French prime minister in September 2005 with the objective of helping young people to become active and useful citizens. Not unlike the CCC, it was launched in conjunction by the ministries of Defense and the Interior and the first centre was opened at Monty in the Departement of Seine-et-Marne on September 30th 2005.

Each year 800,000 young French people participate in the *Journee d'Appel* of which 60,000 are experiencing learning difficulties and 20,000 could be classified in the 'status zero' category mentioned earlier. The aim is to engage with this lowest group by taking volunteers from young people in the age group of 18 to 21 for a period that can last from six months to two years. They wear uniforms.

The first six months are spent in remedial work, both physical and educational, to bring them up to a general standard of competence with a routine similar to that of young soldiers. The next six months they are taught a vocational skill in such areas as the hotel trade, personnel services, security, maintenance or in the building trade. It is planned to open two more centres. This is an excellent programme that satisfies some of the main criteria of what is needed, such as helping to make young people into healthy and useful citizens with a working education. However unlike the CCC, it lacks continuity of dealing with unemployment which, at around 25%, is particularly high among the under 25s in France.

The Swiss Army

The Swiss Army is a unique force that emerged from the history of the republic when, in 1848, the defence of the country was ceded by the cantons to become a federal responsibility. By law, each person between the ages of 18 and 30 is obliged to undergo military training – although there are a number of exceptions through ill-health, education or reluctance to bear arms. This implies that there are over one and a half million potential recruits, the second largest per capita force after Israel. After referenda, the size of the army is now 220,000 including reservists. There are 3,600 professional staff.

There is an initial training period of 18 to 21 weeks depending on the branch of service when the recruits learn the rudiments of soldiery and are able to use the standard Sig 500 rifle, the Sig automatic pistol and a Stinger hand-held anti-aircraft missile. There are then annual regular range training and equipment checks. All service men and women keep their rifles at home and are issued with a sealed box of fifty rounds for self-defence in case of emergency while joining their units. Remarkably, full mobilisation can be achieved in twelve hours – compared with weeks for the United States National Guard. This has only been ordered three times in relatively modern times: in 1870, and during two world wars.

There are penalties for not joining up. The dissidents are obliged to pay an additional 3% on their income tax and serve in Civil Protection which can mean the police, fire department, social service, environmental work, helping the elderly and so on. They also have to spend 50% more time than their military colleagues.

In Summary

We now have a pattern of past and present working ingredients for proposals, some of which meet the objectives set out earlier:

- The Defence 2eme Chance targets a similar age-group to the CCC. This is an excellent initiative but probably lacks continuity for an individual as they get older and should be able to fit into a larger and continuous programme such as NRA described below.

- The example of the Swiss Army has the virtue of being continuous and should form part of the overall plan.

- The National Trust and TCV already exist to provide work, training and any programme should be grafted on to their work

- The CCC provides an excellent template for dealing with a very large problem but there should be no age limit.

Let us call the new organisation...

The Conservation and Security Agency (CSA)

This proposed organisation is designed to put to work the unemployed and those not totally disabled (whose numbers are around 6% of those of working age in the UK); in fact anyone who wants to claim benefit, or as a condition for receiving state-paid insurance, who might be sent to do community service. As a matter of principle it should make the maximum use of those of pensionable age who would wish to increase their income to act either as participants or instructors – just as did the LEMs in the CCC.

It would have the secondary objective of giving fundamental skills to those left behind by the state education system, and to prepare those who want to become self-employed. Once a skill has been learned, the CSA could act as an umbrella organisation – or agency – for the newly independent individuals to earn money by employing the trades set out in the next chapter. Anyone can leave at any time for employment when their support will stop. There will be no pay without work.

Putting the Unemployed to Work

Putting the unemployed to work must form part of any programme aimed to effect the transfer to the Digital Age where many individuals will feel displaced and need re-training. It should also aim to attract individuals such as volunteers or retired specialists who would want to pass on their skills or increase their income by acting as trainers or supervisors; they could also be participants. Its task would be to enrol and give training to all that were claiming state benefit except those who are exempt with young children. After initial aptitude and medical screening tests, individuals would be guided into three levels of participation:

- Local projects connected with the environment, helping needy people and working with the security agencies.

- National disaster relief and helping with infrastructure projects.

- Quasi-military and overseas disaster relief.

Local projects

These imply that the individuals would live locally and could expect to go home after a day's work. They would be managed by the local council and paid a flat rate but there would be additions for taking responsibility, specialist training for fire or flood outbreaks, disease containment, dangerous work or for particular tasks. Where possible they would be seconded to organisations such as the National Trust or TCV. Otherwise, their work would include:

- Helping with county-based organisations involved in preserving heritage by tending sites that are of ecclesiastical, military, industrial, historical, environmental and other interests.

- To support the authorities in their measures to contain pandemics such as helping to bring essential supplies to those most affected.

- To expand the work of the TCV-style work into many rural and urban areas.

- In conjunction with the police, provide Guardian Angel type patrols on public transport, playgrounds, schools, drug-ridden or violent streets and so on. They would be connected to the police radio networks.

- To assist old people with tasks such as shopping, home decorating and possibly companionship.

- To support the National Recovery Agency (NRA) – set out later – through organising crèches, helping to manage the units and so on.

- To form local intelligence either openly or through the internet on the lines of Vigil in the UK and others in the US that help to increase national security, unearth paedophiles, uncover terrorist plots or reveal those plotting crimes. This would be an excellent avenue for those with a less mobile disability.

- Time would be made available, where necessary, for remedial writing, maths and basic subjects.

- There would training for trades and self-employment for those likely to work for themselves; there would be many occasions where those of pensionable age could help with vocational training.

Like the CCC the participants may need conditioning to bring them up to a standard of fitness and would wear a uniform on active duty.

They would be paid weekly by the employing organisation who could also claim a training allowance that various governments spend on varying degrees from 0.5% of GDP up to 1.8%; there would be deductions for poor behaviour, timekeeping or slacking. They could also reward merit and for taking responsibility.

National Disaster Relief

This would raise the level of work to the national tasks undertaken by the CCC. They could live away from home and be specially trained, supervised and paid for national disaster relief; they would be organised by the armed services. Their work would include:

- Taking action to prevent fires by digging fire-breaks, clearing undergrowth and so on. They might also support the fire brigade in firefighting.

- Reviving national networks such as canals, railways, paths or bridleways.

- Flood relief.

- Assisting the authorities with disasters including giving first aid, repairing buildings and levees, clearing rubble, establishing water or electricity supplies, creating sites for the survivors and so on.

They too would wear uniform and be paid a premium for their skills and risks. In addition to receiving specific vocational training, there would be the opportunity for a much wider academic syllabus.

International Relief

This could become the quasi-military counterpoint to the Swiss Army described earlier. They would undertake basic military and extensive training in disaster such as flooding, earthquake or tsunami relief and be available for peace-keeping duties now undertaken by the regular or auxiliary armies; for this they would be under military discipline.

At times they could be merged with the National Disaster Group. However, their primary role would be to help with international relief and with assisting with resettling refugees such as those from Libya, Syria and Afghanistan. This would form a useful training ground for the regular armed forces.

Funding

Apart from the normal unemployment benefit there would be extras for TCV type of work and where local groups would wish to reward the work done. They could employ barter-style payments such as those offered by the Local Exchange Trading system (LETS) first started in British Columbia by Michael Linton.

The original LETS worked with a currency that Linton called a 'green dollar'. The providers included such services as domestic help, provision of food and clothing, baby-sitting, building, gardening and interior design; all these are recorded in a directory that is widely circulated. When work is required the buyer contacts an individual providing the service and the fee is agreed; once done a transaction note is completed and the provider credited with the fee less a small percentage for running the system. The credit can now be spent with others in the directory. Latterly more business-style work has been added such as transport, office work, language and translation services and so on.

A practical example of how 'time dollar' tokens might be used is given by a social health organisation called Elderplan in Brooklyn that is supported by local firms that offered to take the tokens. This project pays credits to over a thousand volunteers who work helping old people with shopping, home decoration, taking them to surgeries, organising self-help groups and caring for the bereaved. The programme has the public backing of politicians and local authorities.

The CSA takes account of society's needs to protect itself, find useful work for its young people, lower crime generated through boredom or idleness and help to educate those for whom the school system has failed. There is the further group: the children from families or single people who contribute to the unacceptable pool of 'status zero' children.

National Recovery Agency

The NRA is modern equivalent of the Elizabethan programme designed to rescue those 'status zero' children, teenagers and adults who represent such a disgraceful failure on behalf of society as a whole. Like the CCC, and Defense 2eme Chance, we must look to the military to provide the ordered structure for helping these people back into the mainstream. There are many skilled people who could help:

- There are skills provided by the modern equivalent of the Local Experienced Men (LEMs) that taught the young men in the CCC. Many of these might be retired carpenters, electricians, builders, gamekeepers, farmers, gardeners, ex-servicemen, nurses, carers, countrymen and so on who could be pleased to help.

- There will be a number in the CSA programme who would have the skills to lead groups, provide skills, help in the administration and so on.

- There could be support from local sports clubs to provide regular training for activity badges.

It is likely that the work of the NRA would attract a number of people from churches, social groups, charitable organisations, local firms and the like who would be happy to assist in such a worthwhile programme. Having considered the underclass there are still many people who need to be helped back into society.

Introducing a local W2-type programme, as described in the *Global Recovery Manual**, the aim would be to bring back into society those who had become left behind and with little hope of entering the constructive mainstream and to meet certain goals.

Chapter 2.
New Opportunities for Individual Employment and Investment

Summary

The present powerful deflationary forces will at some point have to be lanced through a process of debt destruction, probably through inflation, a highly destructive dynamic that will destroy creditors and debtors alike. The scale of the credit holocaust will take with it many of the major banks, finance houses and creditors to sponsor the creation of a quite different method of funding for future enterprises. There will be many opportunities from companies obliged to unwind a swathe of assets to remain solvent and to repair ravaged balance sheets; added to that will be the creation of several levels of support from privatizing the welfare state as too expensive to maintain. This chapter considers how investors can buy in to a great number of new enterprises and so launch a new era of self-employment.

Introduction

The individual will be the biggest winner and heaviest loser in the passage through the very difficult time described in the Introduction, and a process of individual recovery was outlined in the last chapter. The outright winners will be the top 5% able to see advantage in any diversity to create new entities, ideas and opportunities. As was suggested, there would need to be a large support operation, but there will still be left a very large minority who will be obliged to work for themselves for, in a regime of strict economy, politicians will no longer afford to pay them to be idle.

Inadvertently they will have created a powerful new force described in this handbook which is to emphasize the growth in power, accomplishment and importance of the individual, not just in economic, but also in political and social terms. This will be within a much more fluid society where once a person could only air their ideas politically either directly or through the media, the internet has now provided an unrivalled platform; it gives them the power to vote, give their views on a number of issues, provide information, ideas, directions or promote their services in a way unimagined by previous generations.

This new sense of liberty is one of the central themes of this handbook which examines how the environment of the early decades of the 21st century can bring new hope to many – irrespective of their age – who may have felt that life was over after they had been made redundant. This chapter suggests some of the training, employment and investment opportunities that will open up for the Digital Individual.

The transition could be difficult for a large minority who can look forward to a lower regular income which, to an extent, was covered by the measures set out in Chapter 1. However, technological and economic changes will largely alter the face of business in both manufacturing and services. These will range from unwinding the welfare state to many different new enterprises which suggest several layers of new self-employment – there will undoubtedly be many more.

Fluidity in Abilities

One of the advantages for the Digital Individual (DI) is that the new era will encourage a greater fluidity in abilities, particularly those from lower incomes levels. Although there will be a wide gap in wealth, there will be a greater respect for ability at any level because each will be able to make a significant contribution. The categories set out in the Introduction are expanded here, but undoubtedly there will be great interaction and movement between them:

Level A. There will be those employed in the CSA (described in Chapter 1) who have no wish to go out on their own, but many will thrive within a communal environment.

Level B. These will be the new self-employed who have little or no work or business experience but who will emerge from the CSA with the will, skill and energy to work for themselves. They may, however use the CSA as an agency.

Level C. These will be the previous supervisors who were so essential to the proper functioning of the industrial system but will be less needed in a structure of a larger number of more specialised smaller concerns. They will be the flux that enables those at Level B to function and grow and probably form the nucleus of a new grouping of para-professionals.

Level D. Will include the previously well-paid managers and civil servants – who could have expected to climb the corporate ladder – but will now be obliged seek a new independence. Like other grades they will be wise to join the CSA to become re-orientated until they identify their future career which will be in the higher echelons of the self-employed.

These are just some of the techniques helping to create the new self-employed.

Some Specialisations for the Newly Independent to Learn a Skill

The breaking-down activities that were previously the work of a craftsman was the brain-child of F W Taylor, an American engineer who devised the mass-production for Henry Ford's Model T; US industry used the same principle to totally out-class the Axis powers during the Second World War.

Taylor used the concept of breaking down a task, that previously required great skill, into a series of operations that could be learned quite quickly by semi-skilled people and the result would be a finished quality article.

There are now a large minority of people in many countries who have never worked for themselves but who the state can no longer afford to keep idle. They could be taught a simple trade. Applying Taylor's principle, unskilled people could be taught a sub-set of a service that would previously be only open to those with a longer training. For example:

- Gardening could be broken down into lawn mowing and care, growing vegetables, hedge making and maintaining, flower bed preparation and planting and so on.

- A similar line of thought could apply to aspects of carpentry, plumbing, electrical work, building and the like.

- Nursing at present requires a long training but small first aid units locally could be set up to tend to cuts and bruises. They might deal with simple ailments or using a simple monitor to register symptoms before passing the patient onto a professional.

While these may be taught separately individuals could invest in a portfolio of skills and any small investor could help fund these new activities through venture capital agencies – possibly within an umbrella organisations such as the TCV described in the previous chapter. Quite often these could be taught to those working within the CSA and these packages should include training for winning business, bookkeeping, preparing an invoice, banking and the like before working independently.

These are the mechanical skills, but by far the most important attributes of those wishing to gain repeat business as a self-employed person are those of courtesy, personal rectitude, truth, pride in the ability to deliver, personal appearance and consistency – qualities not normally associated with those on government support! Initially there would need to be supervisory help from specialised groups modelled on agencies such as On Demand (described later) and recruited probably from individuals in Level C.

The Rise of the Para-Specialist and the Agent

It is likely that venture capital would be needed to fund the new industrial and service structures providing a sub-set of professional services at a lower cost than one who has spent a long training; one such is an ambulance driver able to provide a number of resuscitation techniques on the way to a hospital. These would be particularly valuable to small business start-ups which are unlikely to afford professional fees; instead they would turn to individuals forming boutiques combining several skills. Again funding would be needed for training packages.

Another avenue would be to act as agents and perhaps mentors of the individuals setting up in Level B. An attractive addition to agents would be to offer extra training for the new age demanding flexibility and continuous learning.

Bringing Redundant Managers into Self-Employment

There will be others, previously managers in the public or private sector or graduates without a demand for their skills, who will be looking for other career opportunities. This would be a dangerous group to neglect politically for unless their concerns are addressed, they are the very people historically to vent their anger in revolutions or civil unrest.

The idea would be to extend the apprentice principle to self-employed activities centred around a trade or vocation by creating tax-advantaged skill centres specialising in extensive practical or vocational skills that could be passed on using new technologies. Apart from helping to fund the activity themselves, successful candidates could be offered venture capital for their start-ups. This could be described as a latter-day guild system that could derive from some of the following opportunities.

Unwinding the Public Services

As described in the *Global Recovery Manual**, this will create many openings to provide what might be described as inter-services that were previously supplied centrally. For example, providing a bespoke weather service to individual firms dependent upon the environment directly associated with their affairs such as garden centres.

These will likely be a source of opportunities particularly for the para-services; new niches will appear. For example one could expect para-medicals to set up first-aid boutiques open 24 hours a day using the individuals mentioned earlier to deal with small injuries, so relieving hard pressed A&E hospital departments. One could envisage speciality medical practices undertaking diagnostic and out-patient operations as part of specialisations normally undertaken by hospitals.

Franchising

This is a useful alternative for those put off by the failure-rate for small businesses (which is as high as 75% in the US over three years from start-up). One way of raising the success-rate is to copy an existing successful business; it is also a sound business investment.

This is a method of replicating a successful business through recording its operations in what is known as a format; this is then tried out in one or more pilot schemes where independent individuals can iron out any difficulties. Once a successful programme has been perfected it is offered to potential franchisees who pays a fee for help in starting up a new business and a royalty on sales. An example of a successful franchise is set out at the end of the chapter. The advantages to both parties are:

- The franchisor receives an ability to expand the business without investing in more staff or assets.

- The franchisee benefits from having a proved and tested business with continued support and help with promotion.

The principle can be applied in reverse by franchising previously owned shops, depots and some manufacturing finishing operations. The process entails making them independent by selling them to the existing management but at the same time keeping the business name and activities; the new owners know the business and their customers and often see an expansion of their operations – 20% is common.

This can be a great advantage to the head office that can look forward to reducing a number of head-office expenses and strengthening the balance sheets from the sale of assets; some examples are set out in *Handbook for Reducing the Break-Even Point***. It is likely that retail chains such as Woolworth, HMV and BHS could have been saved in this way by selling marginal or loss-making stores that can be turned around by enterprising owner managers. The

Handbook contains practical measures of carrying out the process as well as franchising an existing business. This is a simple example:

A family business provides training videos for their clients for training and promotion purposes; there needs to be sufficient margins to provide a royalty. The techniques could be then recorded by a franchise consultant into a format that could be learned by others. The next stage is a pilot testing to prove the procedures before these are offered to non-competing third parties; the merits of the arrangement have been set out earlier.

Some Future Opportunities and Investment Vehicles

Retirement

Retiring becomes less of an option when the ability of the state to support those over 65 reduces and private pensions become less valuable through politically inspired currency devaluations. This presents individuals, and those employing them, with a number of opportunities to transfer accumulated knowledge and experience, taking into account the older person's increasing reluctance to travel and also to tire more quickly. As suggested elsewhere, unwinding the state will provide many opportunities to pass on vocational and other skills to the rising level of the new created self-employed; this would include helping to write franchising formats, bookkeeping, standing in for absences, assisting with administration and so on.

Surprisingly, retirement homes could be centres of enterprise providing extensive skills to the neighbourhood and a means of helping with the fees and keeping people active. Homes could be adapted with particularly specialities such as legal, accounting, property, training or help with administration using modern methods of communication. Others could provide more vocational skills such as carpentry, plumbing, electrical, gardening, tailoring, cookery, nursing or help with children. The services would be locally based and could be complementary to tradesmen or small business people to help with overloads or when the principal is away on holiday.

Professional Boutiques

Professional boutiques comprising several disciplines will become more in vogue with the advent of fewer large, and many smaller companies. These will provide a one-stop accounting, legal, property, architectural and probably other professional services.

Distance Learning

Distance learning in the form of Massive Open Online Courses (MOOCS) will become increasingly popular to provide continuous learning and are already in vogue by some universities offering the ability to participate in lectures remotely but in interactive degree courses. It is intended that the Global Recovery Programme Schools will use this technique increasingly and offer diplomas.

The Home

The home is likely to become a place of business and looking after older generations where each member can make a contribution to preparing meals, answering calls, looking after children and the like. The greater concentration on the home will also apply to health and security where an individual's vital functions will be monitored continuously and downloaded to a home-based computer program and reported to the local medical practice when the signals are outside limits. Homeworking, already in use for many professions, will increase dramatically as the ability to communicate will be such that it will be a regular occurrence for groups to meet remotely;

examples are Go To Meetings where the transferring of documents electronically is routine.

Privatising Schools

Privatising the schools system would provide a great range of schools stretching from the great private and grammar academies to the more humble primary establishments. Many would be offering a much more vocational instruction such as Swiss schools where over one half of pupils learn a trade which accounts for their low unemployment level. The City and Guilds in London already provide wide qualifications but these are likely to be extended. Where once the local school just taught children, it could become a business centre offering specialist training, remedial instruction or a venue for local classes with access to web-based distance learning centres.

Technology and Innovation

As described in Chapter 3, this is the driving force of the Digital Age – just as it was in the early part of the 18th century in England; then it was empirical, now it will be science based although there may well be many spin-offs, just as there were then. While much of it will be research based, engineers will be at a premium, as they were during the 1930s, when innovation to create new products required firms to attract scarce resources. As with medicine, there will be many openings for para-technicians and resources will be needed to train these individual – most probably through apprenticeships.

New Aids to Independence

One can expect new technology-based devices enabling an individual, or small groups, to set up in business to provide bespoke items such as shoes, clothes, windows or furniture. The parameters would be entered into the machine which would then cut out and assemble the product as a finished item.

Centres of Excellence

These will offer apprenticeships to teach new and old technologies with special tax and other advantages. These ideas could be extended to more vocational skills where centres would provide training in trades and be the source of finance from investors and management help for successful graduates. If this was accepted internationally, there would be many opportunities for cross-fertilisation of trades and skills.

Direct Selling

This will provide many openings when suppliers seek to cut out the margin of the wholesaler and retailer. In Japan during the 1990s farmers sold directly to customers. Many will be following the lead of Avon Cosmetics with agents selling such items as clothes, computers and accessories, radios, personal services and the like – see LETS below. This could be accompanied by independent service agents and drones will be used widely to arrange deliveries.

The growing sharing economy such as Uber will mean that assets will become more of an investment.

Direct Costs Reduction Specialists

These specialists will be much in demand as deflation forces many public and private concerns to devolve many routine, and some executive functions. Although this may be impossible for government departments to conceive at present, the need to cut central expenditure will demand higher productivity achieved by hiving these out to the private sector specialist groups. This will reduce the demand for public transportation.

On Demand

The On Demand Programs will help promote the newly created businesses and individual enterprises. These offer either temporary or more durable services at short notice and are useful for the clients but also to those who wish to pursue a number of interests either inside or outside the home. It may also be an attractive way of creating a more permanent position.

Internal Security

Internal security is likely to become a much more community issue with the professional police force more employed in solving crime than in local patrolling. Instead individuals can train to provide a local service such as the Guardian Angels, see Chapter 1, and connected to local police forces on their radio networks. Cyber security, described in the next chapter, will rise in importance.

Careers in Banking and Finance

These could be very different from today's working in big national organisations – few of which are likely to survive the severe deflationary forces hitting highly leveraged nations. Instead banking, and its associated venture capitalism, is likely to return to its roots funded by wealthy individuals aiming to serve a town, county or state. It will be locally driven to help local enterprises at all levels of capital requirement.

Politics on the Swiss model

As described in Chapter 5, this will be much more local in character with national assemblies being composed of part-time delegates with only a few full-time elected officials. They would head the great departments of state such as the treasury, internal security, maintaining the laws of the country, external defence and foreign affairs.

There will, however, be more important local assemblies than at present managing affairs that were previously the responsibility of central government and those more directly associated with people. Like the Swiss cantons, these will vie for incoming business by providing the best educational, social, cultural and tax friendly environment. There would also be extensive consultation both at national and local level by increasing use of referendums.

Faith

The rise of faith usually accompanies difficult times when people are often disorientated by rapidly changing circumstances and are attracted to beliefs and strengths outside themselves. Clerics will be much needed in the newly self-employed support groups.

The Unwinding of the State

The unwinding of the state will increase the need for the voluntary sector that already plays an important part within the English-Speaking Peoples. A further pointer to a return to a more thoughtful period is a loose cycle of around 630 years when the ideas of the great Greek philosopher Plato attract a rising following. We are approaching such a period now.

Annex to Chapter 2:
A Practical Example of Franchising

One such is the Dwyer Group of Waco, Texas that was started by Don Dwyer in 1980. The first venture was a carpet cleaning and dyeing business that, after a successful pilot scheme, generated a number of franchisees.

The Dwyer Group believes in the principle of 'multiplication' whereby their franchisees are offered different products to be sold to the same customers. For example, the portfolio includes a drain-cleaning and plumbing service, a refurbisher of bathroom fittings and a Mr Electric franchise. This is a maintenance plan that has been nominated by the makers of ceiling fans, indoor and outdoor lighting, current-surge protectors and service-panel installations and upgrades.

There is a franchise fee and the royalty on sales varies between 3 and 6% depending on volume. Apart from working for themselves, Dwyer offer a business person a package whereby they can manage several individuals working as employees.

There are already many franchises offered by the *International Franchise Organisation Handbook* but also the possibility that many other different and innovative business could be franchised. One such list has been drawn up the Local Enterprise Agency of Newcastle-on-Tyne in England which has created Business Opportunity Profiles of some 200 new activities – many of which might be franchised.

Chapter 3.
Technology Investment Driving the Digital Age

Summary

Iron, coal and other metals drove the Industrial Era which created an unimaginable range of products that gave riches to a number of people and a livelihood to millions. It concentrated first productive power, then financial and a military authority that in the hands of unscrupulous politicians created wars of expansion. The financial institutions that arose created great wealth for both shrewd participants and investors.

The Digital Age will create quite a new kind of technology and investment opportunities centred around the atom and its limitless applications. Unlike the large corporations of the Industrial Era, the new enterprises are likely to be much smaller, more specific and probably also less durable for rapid advances will make many technologies redundant. In an age when many of the financial institutions will have either disappeared or been replaced by IT, many new and specialist vehicles will grow up to provide investors with opportunities in the new era. These are just some of the present technologies, many more will arise.

Introduction

Carbon and its compounds are the basis for organic chemistry but there exist 200,000 inorganic applications whose properties are not yet known; one application is its use in fixture-free construction. The process begins by creating fine strands some millionth of a metre thick which are then heated and bound into fibre before being woven into sheets that are ready for production. By orientating these sheets and cementing them into place in an automatic process great strength is achieved in assemblies such as Boeing and Airbus aircraft where they comprise half the weight.

The process is also being used for cars and other structures where considerable strength and weight is a premium but the process is becoming cheaper and faster to be adapted to the mass-production of vehicles. The production process is also much simpler for no fasteners such as bolts or rivets are used. Among the very many other uses of carbon is graphene, a film of atoms thick, which has great strength and conductivity; it has many applications including solar power, and minute carbon tubes are being increasingly used for desalination.

Biotechnology

Another carbon based technology is Biotechnology, a process for adapting live organisms for medicine. The process has ancient roots when certain plants were domesticated then used as curatives or other practical means. The story is told of Chaim Weizmann, a professor of chemistry at Manchester, who invented a process for producing acetone from starch during the First World War – so saving many trees in the production of explosives. These are just some of the applications:

- Pharmacology can now prepare treatments adapted for each individual.

- Individual complaints such as cancers, arthritis and hepatitis, among others, can now be targeted by identifying and isolating the errant cell to prevent it from spreading.

- DNA analysis enables harmful genes to be identified then a curative gene spliced into the patient's genetic make-up.

- Live organisms may be used to isolate elements from their basic ore.

Geoengineering

Geoengineering is concerned with exploring means of reducing man-made carbon dioxide by such means as stimulating plankton to absorb more of the gas and other more well-tried methods such as tree planting.

Agriculture

Agriculture took great strides ahead after the Second World War with the 'Green Revolution' which greatly improved the use of hybrids, new methods of cultivation and harvesting, extending the use of aquifers and so on. However, most of these benefits have been implemented and new generations of cultivation are being introduced such as vertical farming, an aspect of aquaculture where plants are circulated with the required nutrients and climatic control. It is held that this optimises the growing cycle and avoids the great waste associated with bringing material to the market and then into homes.

Technology is also being applied to field operations where whole fields are analysed down to small areas for their optimum growing potential; these can then be individually treated to increase the yields. Agriculture uses 70% of all fresh water available despite around two thirds being lost in evaporation and a fifth lost through run-off; Israeli technology has considerably reduced the losses but this cannot wholly reverse the depletion of aquifers that were such a source of water for the Green Revolution. As a further conservation measure new hybrids have been developed to use brackish water.

Nanotechnology

Nanotechnology, the science of dealing with material a billionth of a metre thick – or seven hydrogen atoms wide – has so far been applied to such things as protection against corrosion, surface protection and solar creams. However, its true potential has yet to be realised in fabricating complex structures as an entity or even creating food.

Batteries

Another application is in battery technology where lithium, an unstable element, has been responsible for powering a wide range of cell phones, laptops, power tools and the like. Production techniques have reduced the cost to $300 per kWh but this needs to be lowered to $100 to become economical for electric cars. A further application for batteries is their use in housing where electricity can be stored in off-peak periods then either used or fed back into the grid.

Hydrogen and oxygen are the most efficient fuel combination used to power directional rockets in space craft, but their terrestrial application is increasingly with fuel cells. These use the process similar to a battery by generating current to power vehicles; however, the gas needs to be stored, conveyed and used at very high pressures to be economical.

Information Technology and Robotics

Information technology and robotics are increasingly replacing human operations in the way they are able to store, manipulate and manage data; these techniques have already created a revolution in manufacturing where lines of computer-driven robots now assemble devices such as cars, but their application is increasing rapidly. Already driverless cars will become a reality and in the home, machines are able to replace individuals. This is a huge subject but some aspects are becoming evident:

- Cybertechnology is a growing threat with its ability not just to steal data but to totally disrupt utilities on the scale of wartime; already the Iranian uranium purification gas centrifuge programme was severely disorganised through clever hacking, and nations have been attacked by totally overloading key state functions. To counter this threat billions of dollars need to be spent to foil the attackers.

- The speed of computing power of doubling every 18 to 24 months and its cost remaining static (according to Moore's Law) is coming to the end of its power to innovate. One solution is thought to be quantum computing. Instead of classical computing handling bits very fast, quantum machines use the power of electrons to manage many functions at the same time so speeding up the process immeasurably. It also uses another growing technology of cryogenics which enables materials to be superconductors at very low temperatures.

3D Printing

Additive manufacturing – or 3D Printing – uses the same principle of a laser printer depositing ink but now adds metals or other materials in multiple layers. The system uses a bed onto which a layer of material is deposited according to a predetermined program; once done, the bed is lowered fractionally when another layer is put down and fused into place and the process continues until completion. Although slower than other methods such as injection moulding, the process lends itself to a wide range of different materials which make it ideal when specific or complicated shapes are needed without lengthy machining.

Chapter 4.
The New Corporation

Background

Before the industrial revolution most people worked for themselves in the sense they were paid for the work done and very few, except those in government or in the armed services, were salaried. For many this was a hard life and anything earned was immediately spent on the bare essentials; however in England, in the early 17th century, there was a form of poor relief organised locally by the church wardens. The supplicants were put to work in the fields while their children were made apprentices.

The advent of centralised power, first from the mill stream then steam engines, changed this, enabling hundreds of the newly invented spinning jenny and weaving machines driven by steam engines and operated continuously under one roof; those who had spent their apprenticeships learning how to do this manually were made redundant and had to retrain.

As the industrial revolution spread new towns were created either around a suitable climate, a source of raw materials or a market and two classes of workers emerged. The first were the craftsmen who knew how the machines were built and worked, and could fix them if they went wrong; the second were the operatives, mostly women and children, who were taught one task and spent many hours operating it for a pittance. However, it was a regular income and hordes of families left the countryside for the rapidly built new towns. Only the more enlightened bosses created health and amenity support for their people.

The first to conceive of the big corporation was John D Rockefeller after the first discovery of oil in the United States. Initially the market was for kerosene and highly innovative methods were used to promote the product by offering cheap lamps. However, it was the genius of Henry Ford to perceive that a mass-produced automobile could also create a wide market for accessible transport and the demand for gasoline rocketed. As organisations grew there was a need for professional managers and the first business school in the US was opened at Wharton in the University of Pennsylvania in 1881; later Harvard offered the Master of Business Administration (MBA) to successful graduates.

Other large organisations such as General Motors followed but the anti-trust legislation of Theodore Roosevelt and later aggressive trade unions were to complicate the task of managing large corporations and the demand for professional managers grew, as did business gurus such as Peter Drucker.

Running a business in the Great Depression was not easy but the genius of Alfred Sloan ensured that General Motors not only grew but diversified into areas such as diesel locomotives, aero engines and refrigerators. Britain was late coming to the large corporation but under the wise economic management of Neville Chamberlain a wide variety of manufacturing activities were started in areas such as transportation, aircraft and aero engines, domestic appliances, electronics and the like.

The Second World War saw a demand for millions of competent production managers which, with the support of governments, enabled the allies to totally out-produce the Axis; but wars are also inflationary and many company balance sheets did not reflect the changing values – particularly real estate. This created a quite different type of business chief, the corporate raider after the war, whose plan was to take over companies, realise the underperforming assets then move on. The process was known as asset-stripping and the new corporate entities were known as conglomerates on the principle that good managers should be able to run any business.

They were also prey to management consultants peddling the latest elixir to success.

While the general rise in prosperity with new technology helped to make the work easier, it made it cheaper for much manufacturing and some services to be resourced overseas which coincided with Deng's opening China for capitalism. Quite soon, the giant American store Walmart was buying 10% of China's exports and purchasing from home dwindled.

By the turn of the century when computers, robotics and offshore purchasing were reducing the manufacturing employment of developed countries, another major threat – that of the economic headwinds described in the Introduction and the *Manual of Global Recovery** – was starting which accelerated the changes taking place. By the second decade, rising costs in China were encouraging a return of manufacturing to the West.

A Revolution in Manufacturing

This was only the start of a revolution in manufacturing and employment in the Anglosphere and elsewhere which would change the work patterns away from those that had grown up in the previous century. In particular information technology and robotics are reducing the size of the workplace and opportunities for regular employment accompanied by deflation demanding a reduction of costs; it is also allowing a great devolution of skills.

But this is just the start for the huge range of opportunities and skills released from the new occupations described in the previous chapter will demand the greatest possible flexibility of incorporations that could fall broadly into three categories – although variations will arise:

- There will be many fewer of the large listed companies, and those that remain will be the major process industries. It is unlikely that many conglomerates, even those devoted to a specific industry, will survive the anticipated downturn in business as the directors will often be obliged to sell subsidiaries to the managers to redress leveraged balance sheets by raising funds. Events will also change investment opportunities from stock markets to newly formed venture capital funds

- As a counterpoint to the decline of the listed company very many more will chose to remain owned and developed by the managers who will probably wish to pass enterprises on to their families and descendants which was the common practice in Victorian times. Highly innovative firms will still be targets for predators but, in the anticipated much devolved political structures described in the next chapter, these will seek to become much more part of the community such as the style of the Quaker owned firm of Cadbury.

- The third and most often used will be a limited partnership that can be easily formed and re-formed to suit the needs of what could be fast-moving markets and technologies. This will be similar to the concept of latter-day guilds described in a previous chapter.

We can now discern the different ways in which business is being operated, listed in no particular order of importance:

Direct Selling

This could make many retailers redundant. For example, Amazon has obliged the book and other trades to become much more specialised and to use the Internet to promote their activities; one could see many new stores offering bespoke learning – and even employment introduction – services to support their trade. Often potential purchasers can search and decide on an item such as a car then make a deal with a distributor for service and an agreed price.

Bespoke Items

These will be increasingly in demand and be satisfied by new computer-driven devices where the dimensions of a shoe, dress or item of furniture can be entered into a program to produce much or all of a finished article.

Company Size

The size of many new companies will be smaller than previously using technology manned by specialists to either sell directly or as sub-contractors such as the German *Mittelstand*. As suggested in a previous chapter, this will release many of the present middle managers and supervisors who will demand the extensive employment and investment opportunities from unwinding the public and private institutions suggested in the next chapter.

Innovation

Innovation will become an essential ingredient to make engineers and technicians more valuable than accountants and lawyers in a deflationary environment where buyers will be attracted to new features rather than wait until an item is cheaper. This will continue into the Digital Era.

There will be many variations offered on a common theme. For example a basic item such as a car or motor bicycle will be offered with many different features such as colour, trim, engine size, amenities, comfort and the like.

Fixed Variable Costs

Converting fixed to variable costs to lower the break-even point will be an essential feature of weathering any downturn which will mean sub-contracting much of the routine work that cannot be undertaken by robotics or IT programs. This will give rise to specialist groups or individuals offering a service that can be located anywhere.

The concept of sub-contracting can apply to such things as design, promotion, manufacture, shipping, invoicing and payment collection whereby a major operation can be managed by a relatively few key staff.

Supporting Services

Supporting services for CEOs will include virtual boards which can provide intelligence on factors affecting the security and success of a business to include such matters as markets, commodities, weather, economics, currencies and the like. They will be offered by specialist individuals who know the business and the environment in which it works. They might be situated anywhere to provide CEOs with regular reports and, if necessary, oblige the enterprise to adapt their agendas for rapidly moving markets and demands.

An extension of this idea could be 'company health checks' whereby a board would be invited to address a number of different situations, and their decisions quantified financially. This would have been highly beneficial in the difficult trading situation that many companies found themselves in the 1970s; one such company in the wallpaper business failed to adapt to the rapid changes in costs and markets by keeping to a routine of quarterly board meetings; it subsequently failed.

Product Testing

This will be greatly simplified through the use of 3D Printing described in the previous chapter. This can be used from the computer design stage to produce an article then offer it to selected users for evaluation and, if necessary, modification before being more widely offered for sale.

Entry Costs

Entry costs for new products or services are being much reduced through the opportunity to promote these on the net. Electronic addresses of groups of potential customers are becoming very valuable as a marketing tool.

Start-Up Services

These will become increasingly in demand to include such matters as helping with a name, creating an identity, arranging a web site, providing introduction to promotion services; this could also include suggesting sources of financing and the like. The principle could be applied to the On Demand agencies suggested in Chapter 2 or through para-professional partnerships suggested later.

Renting Cars

This is already an established business but the rise of firms like Uber make the process more flexible and less structured. The same would be true of Airbnb renting properties, more expensive garden equipment and the like.

Retraining

Retraining will become much more significant in a rapidly changing working environment where individuals will wish, or be obliged, to change direction several times.

Finance

Finance has been traditionally provided through banks, stock markets or venture capitalists. However, with the likely collapse of many banks and financial institutions, wealthy private individuals will be increasingly seeking new ventures. The new para-professional partnerships described in an earlier chapter could be a useful entry point.

Associations of the Self-Employed

These will become a potent social, wealth and political force just as the guilds in the 17th century; they will be in a position to demand the lifting of restrictions or initiating sympathetic legislation. This is covered in more detail in the next chapter.

Financing Structures

These have been mentioned earlier as a means to retain the combination of ownership and management in new ventures. However, as the demand for finance increases, it is likely to become more regional in nature from agencies funded by individuals or by other associations. In this way there will a closer relationship between the company, its managers and its owners.

Chapter 5.
The Structures of the
New Paradigm

...Behold I make all things New
Revelations Chapter 21

Summary

This handbook has described many of the features that emerged from dismantling the present Industrial Era – and its transition to the Digital Age. It has meant unwinding the state superstructures that well-meaning politicians built while attempting to provide their voters with free services of health, education and welfare with apparently no understanding of how it would be funded in difficult times – or when things went wrong. Instead when taxation no longer paid for their largess they resorted to borrowings; this is without any regard that over 80 years ago the need to collapse many national and private borrowings – more than half the present levels – caused the greatest slump in history.

This process is set out in the *Global Recovery Manual**; now we have to look ahead for the purpose of this handbook is to identify how the decisions taken now would morph, or even be relevant, into the Digital Age (DA). Knowing what we do of the trends these are some of the most likely outcomes – but, in a devolved age, many more will be attempted.

Introduction

We have seen that a totally different mindset is needed by politicians when a large minority of the population will be working for themselves; this is not counting those of pensionable age whose incomes have been destroyed by the deliberate reduction of fiat currencies. Instead of building empires to manage services, those in power will be obliged to create the optimum devolved structures to encourage entrepreneurs and business people to invest, hire help and employ services.

It is the start of a bottom-up approach to organising working and social life and politics, spurred on by the rise of the Virtual and Sharing Community. Instant communication now allows groups, probably taking resources from all over the world, to form enterprises in the most propitious regions offering the optimum tax, social, cultural, educational and pleasant environments. Many will want to stay there; others, having completed their mission, could then dissolve their arrangements and the entrepreneurs then reform with possibly quite different partners elsewhere.

The Rise of the Individual

The theme of this handbook has emphasised the rising domination of the individual, how they would work and be funded; we can consider their impact on at least three levels; state, corporate and themselves.

State

It has been suggested that the new self-employed, and those of pensionable age who have lost their income through currency devaluation, will form a formidable constituency. They will elect politicians sympathetic to their cause which, in a much simplified central government, will demand acceptable policies and tax structures; it will be up to their equivalent in the regions or states to provide the equivalent service. It will almost certainly mean the end of present political parties because any policies would need to be subject to wide consultation through the instant communications of the new virtual age. Differences now will be no longer political but about how much money can be left in the pocket of their constituents and the substance of any law enacted.

Now those who aspire to lead nations will be more like wise consultants, good shepherds and sages with something of the warrior who propose ideas and policies. They will live in an era when the new self-employed will form associations with those in other nations, for there will be much cross-fertilisation of ideas and techniques. These will be reflected in foreign policies which will mitigate, to an extent, the strife that has been a feature of equivalent periods in history set out in the Introduction. Their warrior qualities will need to deal with these.

At lower levels in the process of devolving of activities to local government one could expect small towns or village levels to be much more self-contained on the lines of the Swiss communes or Israeli Kibbutz described in the Addendum; this also describes some successful educational and medical models that might be adapted to suit local circumstances.

Some services such as libraries could become child care centres with the help of those in one of the CSA groups described in Chapter 1. Others may employ para-specialists who might live locally to organise such matters as policing, road and other maintenance, rubbish collection, basic medical and welfare services and the like. The unwinding of the welfare state will create a number of support services that were either not provided at all or offered in a different way that will enrich life at all levels of activity; for example, schools could become centres of retraining for those whose talents were no longer marketable.

Corporate

The previous chapter set out the likely features of the new business structures, for we are entering a period of very rapid change where the rate of innovation and obsolescence will be high; like the Swiss cantons, regions will seek to attract the smartest entrepreneurs who, as suggested earlier, will demand the most propitious business, cultural and personally pleasing environment.

These are individuals who Chapter 2 described as the deal makers who would thrive in even the most difficult business conditions, and who comprise perhaps 5% of the population. They will also need the more conventional business people whose requirements, described in the last chapter, will be also be paramount.

All these will need the quality of supporting business and technical environment found most in the great cities such as London and New York – but will need to be replicated, at different levels, elsewhere. One can expect many variations of style and supporting services to satisfy the extraordinary range of activities that will spring up.

While the Industrial Era concentrated activities firstly in sources of physical power, then in financial and technical expertise and markets, the new activities will be much more dispersed around individuals or groups with particular competence and linked by technology. They will be not unlike miniature Silicon Valleys that will revive towns and villages; no longer will young people need to leave for the cities, for each unit will provide their own appropriate supporting social and entertainment – as, in the Victorian Age, much will be home based. New business centres could be located perhaps in a church or pub – where individuals and elected officials will be able to communicate using the latest equipment with customers and suppliers at minimum cost.

It will also markedly increase efficiency for people can work at their own level of activity and there will be much less need for commuter travel which will greatly relieve the transport system and personal strain. Individuals will have more time to give their services to local affairs and for each other.

The Individual

This handbook has been primarily directed towards the measures that need to be taken to ensure a relatively smooth unwinding of the superstructure associated with the Industrial Era and the sort of social and structural arrangement that could emerge. Many, of course, will be still employed, albeit with some change of direction, to find themselves in a much more fluid environment that a number will find uncomfortable.

However, those at the lower end of the society, some of whom have never worked, will greatly resent the fading of state support they had before. To some extent this will be taken care of by the CSA described in Chapter 1 requiring them to work in order to draw any benefit. Possibly the most interesting will be the hardy souls who decide to become self-employed who could be the greatest innovators.

The story is told of a small boy – let's call him Fred – who had the job of working the great beam steam pump engines used to evacuate water in mines. These were very low pressure machines designed by Thomas Newcomen with the power stroke being atmospheric pressure. Fred's first task in the cycle was to open the steam valve admitting pressure to the underside of a large piston surrounded by leather to keep in the pressure.

Once it had reached its upper limit the steam was turned off, a water valve admitted a spray that cooled the steam; this created a part-vacuum which allowed air pressure of nearly 14 pounds per square inch to force the power stroke. It is a matter of history that James Watt did not invent the steam engine, he actually invented the condenser to recycle the hot water and made the piston double-acting – so making the process much more efficient.

One day, probably bored with opening and closing valves, Fred noticed that his motions coincided with the movements of the beam so, with the help of an ingenious blacksmith, they arranged a linkage that would work the valves automatically. They made a fortune by selling the device which speeded-up and reduced the cost of operations.

In the Digital Age there will be many Freds and Fredas who will thrive in a much more fluid society that over time has already created many new entrepreneurs – and even more in the future.

This handbook is dedicated to their success.

Addendum

This handbook has focussed on two major issues: protecting the individual from politically induced deflation, and probably also inflation; it also shows how the forces of emancipation will give them a freedom probably not experienced for centuries. However, as suggested earlier, before this can happen the costly and no longer affordable politically driven welfare state must be unwound and alternatives found. This addendum examines at least three models among the very many that will arise. These are the evolutionary Swiss system, Singaporean Medisave and the Israeli Kibbutzim – all will become models at different ends of the political spectrum.

Switzerland

The Medieval 'Hundred' was the basic unit of administration and is likely to have inspired the highly devolved Swiss system – the commune. The Hundred was originally a unit providing a hundred warriors or a hundred homes described in Tacitus and was practiced in England, Scandinavia, Germany and the USA. The Hundreds organisations was a basic concept of Thomas Jefferson who was much against the centralisation of Alexander Hamilton and existed in some US communities some time later.

In England it obeyed the Common Law and was owned either privately or by the church or manor – and existed as a unit until 1894; its superior unit was the parish and the county and from 1832 it was used to define parliamentary boundaries. The law was administered by twelve freeholders or freemen and met at least once a month and the powers were only transferred to the county in 1867. The Normans used it as a source of revenue; a representative of the king approached each local sheriff – or reeve – to decide how much each should be paid.

It is interesting to review how the 'Hundred' principle devolved in Switzerland, for it morphed into the commune, of which there are 2,900 in 26 cantons; these can consist of from 30 to 10,000 people. This principle is reflected in budgetary expenditures of which the Federal Government takes nearly 32%, the Cantons 41% and the Communes 27%. This implies a unique level of local devolution, leaving the central government only responsible for such matters as internal and external security, the exchequer, foreign affairs, transport policy and administration. There are seven members of the cabinet compared to 26 in Britain. Some examples shows how this works in practice.

Welfare is a commune responsibility which is supportive of individuals such as unmarried mothers or those in need. The funding is from central government and from local taxes which, if people try to take advantage of the system, means unpopular increasing local levies. The incidence of unmarried mothers is 16% compared with 46% in Britain.

A similar system exists for those made redundant; after the state support system runs out, the support is from the commune whose members can easily spot whether individuals are cheating by moonlighting.

Swiss education is primarily the responsibility of the cantons but nursery and primary education is delegated to the communes. After primary schooling, around two thirds go to vocational schools where the training is divided between one and a half days in specialised colleges, the rest being spent with a commercial company to learn practical skills as apprentices and a positive attitude to work; at the successful end of the three year course the apprentice is granted the Federal Capacity Certificate. However, some may gain a Vocational Baccalaureate at a technical college and go on to university.

Around one third go to grammar schools and then on to ten Cantonal universities divided between five German-speaking, four French and one Italian establishment; there are two Federal technical colleges in Zurich and Lausanne. Unlike Britain, and several other countries, there are very few of those described as NEETs (not in education, employment and training) – some 10% of the unemployed in Britain; in addition the level of youth unemployment is 4.5% in Switzerland compared with 25% in France and 50% in Spain!

Healthcare is insurance based to cover treatment and hospitalisation and, although compulsory, several insurance companies compete for taking up to 8% of each person's personal income which can vary depending upon the level of insurance chosen, ie dental care, private rooms and so on – the state pays for excess costs. In addition, the individual pays 10% of the cost of treatment up to a certain limit. The canton is the basic unit of organisation although there are some federal hospitals. Private health care is also available.

While this is excellent by British standards there are several other models such as those practiced in Singapore.

Singapore

This is a government sponsored system based on the principle of minimum administrative cost whereby individuals are treated to a high level of care largely funded by compulsory payroll savings which accumulate and share within a family. The care is then divided; GPs are paid cash for their services and a proportion of the savings go towards an in-patient insurance and there is a means tested support for hospital treatment. In this way much of the bureaucracy common with an all insurance programme is avoided.

The total cost to the state is 5% of GDP and it is rated one of the best in the world.

Israel and the Kibbutz

Most of the first migrants to Israel came from Europe, so the concept of a self-sustaining community could have come from Hundreds, however the development of the kibbutz has been quite different. They were first funded by national Jewry but since 1948, the Israeli government have been supportive for they were an intrinsic part of the original borders of the state and its defence strategy. Unlike the free enterprise of the Swiss commune, the group system of the first settlers was on the socialist principle of 'give all you can, take what you need'. It is included as a model because many variations are likely to be explored in the new devolved structures.

The first kibbutz was founded in 1909 in the harsh environment of the Ottoman Empire when much of Galilee was a swamp and the Judean Hills barren; in addition, much of the land had a salt crust from excessive irrigation which was then a backbreaking task to remove. In 2010 there were 270 kibbutzim accounting for 40% of agricultural and 9% of industrial production.

Many of the communities were religiously based and everything was held in common – even children of married couples were deemed to be a joint responsibility and lived away from their parents. The system flourished during the British Mandate after the First World War and the communities increased in size fed from individuals fleeing the pogroms in Russia and the anti-Semitism of Germany; the latter became a flood after Hitler assumed power in 1933 and the Nuremberg Laws were introduced. The inrush was stemmed after the Arab Revolt in 1938 against further migration.

Inevitably perhaps, the socialist fervour of the initial kibbutz waned as the more successful individuals were not prepared to subsidise the more idle members and demanded private property. Also, as manufacturing industry was introduced, there was a more structured society and more people lived within the group but worked elsewhere – a development which meant Arabs, who could not be members, were hired as farmhands.

The concept of local authority, responsibility and self-support is likely to be a growing theme of the digital era and, although the models described could be used initially, many more will proliferate.

References

* Global Recovery Manual by William Houston (ADVFN 2015)

** Handbook for Reducing the Break-even Point by William Houston (ADVFN 2017)

*** The Future of the Professions by Suskins and Suskins (Oxford 2015)

**** The Sovereign Individual by James Davidson and William Rees-Mogg (Simon and Schuster 1997)

Trust for Conservation Volunteers, www.btcv.org

Civilian Conservation Corps, The – https://en.wikipedia.org/wiki/Civilian_Conservation_Corps

Defense 2eme Chance – www.defense.gouv.fr/sites.defense/enjeux_defense/defense_et_soci ete/armees-national/defense_2eme_chance332

Guardian Angels, The – www.guardianangels.org

Landsman Community Service Ltd, 375 Johnson Avenue, Courtney, British Columbia, V9N 2Y2

National Trust The, Thames and Chiltern Region, Hughenden Manor, High Wycombe, Buckinghamshire HP14 4LA

Swiss Army https://en.wikipedia.org/wiki/Swiss_Armed_Forces

Wisconsin's Make Work W-2 Program

The Industries of the Future by Alec Ross (Simon and Schuster 2016)

ET Magazine

The Economist December 5th 2015, Material Difference

Global Recovery Center www.globalrecoverycenter.org

About the Author

William Houston joined the Royal Navy at the end of the Second World War and specialised in weapons. After leaving the service, he qualified as a chartered engineer and an administrator before embarking on a career as a company recovery specialist either directing or advising a wide range of industrial and commercial concerns. For ten years he was an industrial advisor to a merchant bank before taking up a career in writing. His first book *Avoiding Adversity* was published in 1989 advising managers how to survive the following recession.

He then became interested in the cycles of the world including economics, climate, politics, warfare, disease, and wrote *Riding the Business Cycle*, *Future Storm* and *Water: the Final Resource* – the latter two co-authored with Robin Griffiths, a noted technical analyst and investor.

He subsequently became the principal of The School of Global Recovery.

Previous books:

Avoiding Adversity
Meltdown
Riding the Business Cycle
Future Storm
Water: the Final Resource by Houston & Griffiths (Harriman House 2008)
The Global Recovery Manual
School of Global Recovery
How the United States Recovered
How Britain Recovered
Two Recoveries and Two Re-Orientations
2015 – 2025 The Dark Decade
Handbook for Reducing the Break-even Point
The Digital Age, Empowering the Individual
School of Global Recovery

For further information visit www.globalrecoverycenter.org.

Reviews of William Houston's Other Books

Daily Mail: "Houston's work is fascinating"

The Times: "The Chancellor of the Exchequer might well be advised to lay aside his Treasury briefing paper to read *Meltdown* – the book describes a chilling scenario of worldwide financial collapse, and also functions as a manual to take advantage of the ensuing opportunities."

Financial Times: "William Houston is prepared to be unorthodox and that is important when the green shoots of conventional economic wisdom have proved so misleading."

Lord Rees-Mogg: "I advise all those interested in the future to read *Riding the Business Cycle*."

Bill Meridian of Cycles Research: "*Water: The Final Resource* by William Houston and Robin Griffiths. This easily-readable book presents complex data about the earth and it's precious resource Water. The current trends point towards greater demand and flat to declining supply."

James Puplava, CEO of PFS Group and Host of the Financial Sense News Hour, San Diego, California: "...Two tsunamis, one financial/economic and the other climatic are about to converge and unleash their destructive force upon the world's economy... For investors, *Triple Tsunamis* is your compass to help navigate the troubled time ahead... One of the most thought provoking books I have recently read."

Stephen Hill, CEO of Anglo-Sino Capital Partners: "Bill Houston reflects a lifetime of close observation, induction and erudition. This work has practical lessons for everyone, from the President/Prime Minister down to each of the unemployed."

Spectator Business: "'Water is going to control the political, economic and social agenda over the next twenty years,' Houston says. 'It is going to be the major military issue for the next generation.'"

The Guardian on *Water: the Final Resource*: "...even so, their main topic is an important one – the politics of water usage as it planetary changes. They explain dams, irrigation, water recycling and desalination, and consider future impacts of water on crops and population."

Dr Marc Faber, editor of the *Gloom, Boom and Doom report*: "Mr Houston is right when he says that the economic problems are not 'the only difficulties' facing us. In *Triple Tsunamis* Mr. Houston shows that in future, water and food shortages are likely to bring about conflicts and how they might affect asset markets. Houston's analysis of the 'Immense Forces of Change' is fascinating."

Stephen Lewis, Chief Economist, Monument Securities: "William Houston challenges the prevailing wisdom that governments can lead a nation out of recession. In his latest book, *Triple Tsunamis*, policymakers have not yet begun to come to grips with the root cause of the financial breakdown, the unbridled expansion of debt at all levels of the economy over many years. They are also paying no attention to how changes in weather conditions are likely to affect what is arguably the most important economic question of all, how people are to feed themselves. He sets the challenges facing responsible decision-makers, whether they are running businesses from day to day or are charged, as leaders, with attempting to establish a policy that nurtures enterprise, in the context of the long-term cycles that clearly emerge from the historical record.

There is no reason for despair, Mr Houston maintains. The technological cycle has been one of the most important features of human development. There are striking parallels between the present-day revolution in communications technology and the invention of printing with movable type in the fifteenth-century. Just as the latter facilitated the spread of ideas and waves of innovation in the centuries that followed, so we seem likely now to be on the threshold of another leap forward.

Triple Tsunamis provides an invaluable guide for businessmen and policymakers to the pitfalls that lie ahead and the opportunities that are beckoning in the post-crisis world."

Also by William Houston

The Global Recovery Manual

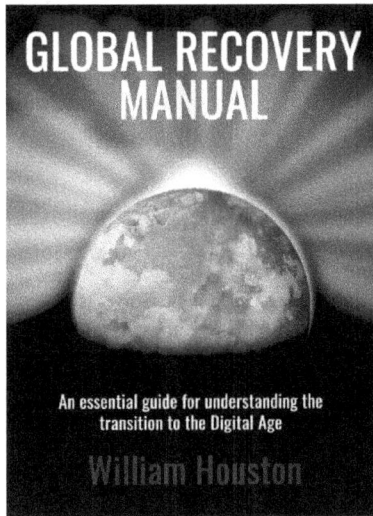

GLOBAL RECOVERY MANUAL

An essential guide for understanding the transition to the Digital Age

William Houston

Markets are in turmoil all over the world. But it's not just the financial markets that are in trouble. The world is suffering some of the greatest natural and man-made imbalances ever, creating a watershed in global affairs that has not been present for centuries. These are driving many people in the Western World into a sense of despair that is endangering their jobs, homes, savings and pensions.

Politicians either don't understand, or don't care, what to do next – they simply 'kick the can down the road' in the vain hope that the danger will either go away or someone else will take responsibility.

The Global Recovery Manual explains how we can get out of the mess and advance into the uplands of the Digital Age.

Available in paperback and for the Kindle from Amazon.

The School of Global Recovery

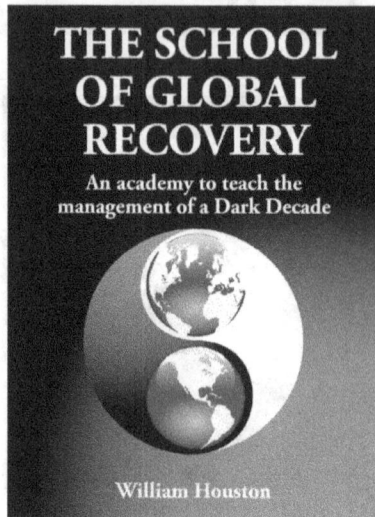

The SOGR was set up to teach how to successfully negotiate a dark decade and manage the transition through to the Digital Age.

The principal of the School, William Houston, explains why the efforts of politicians to balance their books are unlikely to succeed while keeping the present superstructure of the state which has grown at the expense of rising debt. With the world suffering some of the greatest natural and man-made imbalances ever, the result is a watershed in global affairs that has not been present for centuries. These events are driving many people in the Western World into a sense of despair that is endangering their jobs, homes, savings and pensions.

However, through the manageable darkness will emerge the Digital Age when every person will have the possibility of having the dignity of making their own contribution.

The aim of SOGR is to explain how we can get out of the mess and advance into the uplands of the Digital Age. It provides a guide for all those in any sort of authority, setting out courses of action in the hope that a dark age in human affairs may be passed through with the minimum of human suffering.

Available in paperback and for the Kindle from Amazon.

More Books from ADVFN

The Game in Wall Street

by Hoyle and Clem Chambers

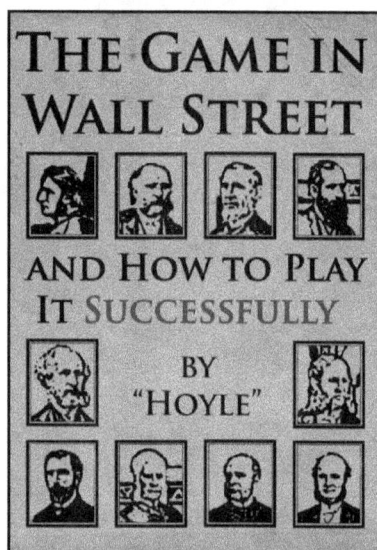

As the new century dawned, Wall Street was a game and the stock market was fixed. Ordinary investors were fleeced by big institutions that manipulated the markets to their own advantage and they had no comeback.

The Game in Wall Street shows the ways that the titans of rampant capitalism operated to make money from any source they could control. Their accumulated funds gave the titans enormous power over the market and allowed them to ensure they won the game.

Traders joining the game without knowing the rules are on a road to ruin. It's like gambling without knowing the rules and with no idea of the odds.

The Game in Wall Street sets out in detail exactly how this market manipulation works and shows how to ride the price movements and make a profit.

And guess what? The rules of the game haven't changed since the book was first published in 1898. You can apply the same strategies in your own investing and avoid losing your shirt by gambling against the professionals.

Illustrated with the very first stock charts ever published, the book contains a new preface and a conclusion by stock market guru Clem Chambers which put the text in the context of how Wall Street operates today.

Available in paperback and for the Kindle from Amazon.

The Death of Wealth

by Clem Chambers

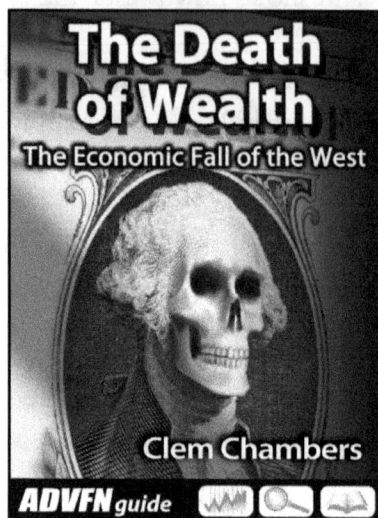

Question: what is the next economic game changer?
Answer: The Death of Wealth.

Market guru Clem Chambers dissects the global economy and the state of the financial markets and lays out the evidence for the death of wealth.

The Death of Wealth flags up the milestones on the route towards impending financial disaster. From the first tentative signs of recovery in the UK and US stock markets at the start of 2012, to the temporary drawing back from the edge of the Fiscal Cliff at the end, the book chronicles the trials and tribulations of the markets throughout the year.

Collecting together articles and essays throughout the last twelve months along with extensive new analysis for 2013, *The Death of Wealth* allows us to look at these tumultuous events collectively and draw a strong conclusion about what the future holds.

2012 started with the US economy showing signs of recovery, and European financial markets recovering some of the ground lost during the euro crisis. It ended with Obama's re-election and the deal that delayed the plunge off the fiscal cliff by a few months.

In between, the eurozone crisis continued, but none of the affected countries actually left the eurozone; quantitative easing tried to turn things around with the consequences of these "unorthodox" actions yet unknown; and the equity markets after the mid-year correction became strongly bullish.

The Death of Wealth takes you through the events of 2012 month by month, with charts showing the movements of the FTSE 100, the NASDAQ COMPX and the SSE COMPX throughout the year.

With an introduction by renowned market commentator and stock tipster Tom Winnifrith and a summary by trading technical analyst Zak Mir, this collection chronicles the rocky road trip the financial systems of the world have been on and predicts the ultimate destination: the death of wealth as we know it.

Available in paperback and for the Kindle from Amazon.

For more information go to the ADVFN Books website at www.advfnbooks.com.

ADVFN BOOKS

www.ingramcontent.com/pod-product-compliance
Lightning Source LLC
Chambersburg PA
CBHW072209270326
41930CB00011B/2590